D0934593

JOE FLACCO

BY MARTY GITLIN

Published by ABDO Publishing Company, PO Box 398166, Minneapolis, MN 55439.
Copyright © 2014 by Abdo Consulting Group, Inc. International copyrights reserved in all
countries. No part of this book may be reproduced in any form without written permission
from the publisher. SportsZone™ is a trademark and logo of ABDO Publishing Company.

Printed in the United States of America,
North Mankato, Minnesota
052013
012014

Editor: Chrös McDougall
Series Designer: Craig Hinton

Photo Credits: Paul Spinelli/AP Images, cover, 1; Jed Jacobsohn/AP Images, 4; Zuma
Press/Icon SMI, 7, 23; Jeff Fusco/Getty Images for Reebok, 8; Sean Brady/WireImage/
Getty Images, 10; Joe Giblin/AP Images, 13; Pamela Kay Schmalenberger/AP Images, 14;
Jim Cowsert/Icon SMI, 16; Aaron Josefczyk/Icon SMI, 19; Ann Heisenfelt/AP Images, 20;
Jay Talbott/Icon SMI, 24; Ric Tapia/Icon SMI, 27; Tony Medina/Icon SMI, 28

Library of Congress Control Number: 2013934739

Cataloging-in-Publication Data
Gitlin, Marty.
 Joe Flacco: Super Bowl MVP / Marty Gitlin.
   p. cm. -- (Playmakers)
ISBN 978-1-61783-699-2
1. Flacco, Joe, 1985- --Juvenile literature. 2. Football players--United States--Biography-
-Juvenile literature. 3. Quarterbacks (Football)--United States--Biography--Juvenile
literature.   I. Title.
796.332092--dc23
[B]   2013934739

TABLE OF CONTENTS

Joe Flacco

CHAPTER 1

QUARTERBACK IN TRAINING

J oe Flacco had proven to be a good quarterback throughout his first five National Football League (NFL) seasons. At Super Bowl XLVII in February 2013, he set out to prove he was a great quarterback.

Joe wasted little time in making his case. He connected with wide receiver Anquan Boldin for an early touchdown. That put the Ravens up 7–0. He then added two more touchdown passes before the half.

Baltimore Ravens quarterback Joe Flacco prepares to take a snap in Super Bowl XLVII.

Baltimore led the San Francisco 49ers 21–6 at halftime. The lead grew to 28–6 after the Ravens returned the second-half kick for a touchdown. The 49ers made a second-half push. But Joe and the Ravens held on to win the championship 34–31. After the game, Joe was named the Most Valuable Player (MVP). Yes, he was indeed great!

Joe had been working toward that moment his entire life. He grew up in the small town of Audubon, New Jersey. There were many athletes in his family. His parents, Steve and Karen Flacco, were high school sweethearts and standout athletes. And both of Joe's grandfathers had played high school football in the 1950s. His parents and grandfathers all went to the same high school in New Jersey.

Audubon is a city of 9,000 people on the border of Pennsylvania. Most football fans there root for the Philadelphia Eagles. Even Joe watched Eagles games when he was growing up. Most of his friends are still Eagles fans. However, many Audubon residents placed Ravens flags outside their homes before Super Bowl XLVII.

Flacco throws a pass against the San Francisco 49ers during the third quarter of Super Bowl XLVII.

Joe is the oldest of six children. He has four brothers and one sister. And like their parents and grandfathers, all of the Flacco children were great athletes. They would brag about their skills at the dinner table. They often played against each other, too. They played basketball at the elementary school. They played Wiffle ball in the backyard. And they played football in the muddy fields near their home.

Joe, *center back*, poses with his family after the Baltimore Ravens selected him in the 2008 NFL Draft.

Joe was a fine baseball pitcher. However, he became an even better football player. It took some time, though. His father did not let him play organized football until seventh grade. By then Joe was growing into his current 6-foot-6 body. That made him a bit clumsy in middle school. Coaches could see great things in Joe's future, though. He could throw the ball with a lot of power and accuracy.

Joe earned playing time as a freshman at Audubon High School. Coach Mark Deal believed that Joe could throw the ball harder than some college quarterbacks.

Audubon's football team struggled. It had losing records during all four of Joe's seasons. But Joe still proved to be a good player. He threw for more than 450 yards and three touchdowns in one game. His team still lost 67–35, though. He also set South Jersey records in another game by completing 37 passes for 471 yards. However, it was another lopsided defeat. Joe never had great team success in high school. But he still said he loved the high school experience.

Joe's positive attitude and quiet confidence helped him blossom on the football field. He also did well in the classroom. And he was about to take his growing talent to the next level.

Joe had four brothers: Michael, John, Brian, and Tom. All have had success in organized sports. Michael plays first base in the Boston Red Sox's minor league system. John is a wide receiver at Stanford University. Brian is a fine second baseman for his community college baseball team. And Tom is a great high school quarterback.

Joe Flacco

CHAPTER 2

BECOMING A BLUE HEN

College scouts took notice of Flacco. They saw how his Audubon High School team struggled. But they did not care. They knew a talented quarterback when they saw one. And many scouts wanted Flacco to play at their schools.

Flacco had three finalists. They were the University of Pittsburgh, Rutgers University, and Virginia Tech. He eventually chose Pittsburgh. Flacco wanted to play for Panthers coach Walt Harris.

Flacco preps his Pittsburgh Panthers teammates before a snap during a 2004 game.

Harris was known for developing great quarterbacks. The relationship began with high hopes. One scout predicted Flacco could become the next Dan Marino. That was incredible praise for a quarterback fresh out of high school. Marino starred with the Panthers during his college days. He later blossomed into one of the greatest quarterbacks in NFL history.

But Flacco was not given a chance to start blossoming at Pittsburgh. He redshirted as a freshman in 2003. That gave him a season to transition to college play. Flacco thought he might become the starter in 2004. But Harris instead selected Tyler Palko for that job. Flacco completed just one pass the entire year. Harris left after that season. The new coach listed Flacco as the third-string quarterback before the 2005 season. His career was going backward.

In 2007, Flacco was named a co-winner of the Colonial Athletic Association Offensive Player of the Year Award. He shared the honor with University of New Hampshire quarterback Ricky Santos. Santos played briefly in the Canadian Football League

Flacco looks to hand off during Delaware's 2006 game against the University of Rhode Island.

That led to a tough decision. Flacco could transfer to another school. But then he would lose his current scholarship. College rules also say transferring players must sit out for a season. However, at Pittsburgh he was just standing on the sideline during games anyway. So he decided to switch schools.

Flacco left to join the University of Delaware Blue Hens. Delaware was not exactly a football powerhouse. But the team

Flacco gets a pass off against Southern Illinois University during the 2007 college football playoffs.

gave Flacco a chance to play. He threw 18 touchdown passes and ran for five more as a junior in 2006. And he was just warming up. He emerged as one of the top quarterbacks in the nation his senior year.

Flacco piled up one brilliant performance after another. In his final college season he had 23 passing touchdowns and only five interceptions. He also rushed for four more touchdowns.

His best game was an offensive showcase against the Naval Academy. Flacco completed 30 of 41 passes for 434 yards. He also had four passing touchdowns. Delaware won the shootout 59–52.

The Blue Hens soared behind Flacco. They finished the season with an 11–4 record. NFL teams were impressed with Flacco's strong arm. But some were scared away by the fact that he played at Delaware. Baltimore Ravens staffers were not expecting much from a pre-draft workout with Flacco. But what they saw was a future star. They were ready to bring him to Baltimore.

Delaware went 5–6 in Flacco's junior year. It improved to 8–3 the next regular season (11–4 overall). One highlight of Flacco's senior year was a playoff win over in-state rival Delaware State University. Flacco threw for 189 yards and one touchdown in the game. Delaware won easily, 44–17.

16   *Joe Flacco*

CHAPTER 3

INTO THE FIRE

Being a quarterback in the NFL is very difficult. So most NFL rookie quarterbacks spend their Sundays on the sideline. Quarterbacks need to be able to read defenses and know when and where to throw the ball. And it often takes a few seasons to fully understand the complexities of the position.

But Flacco had no time for that in 2008. Kyle Boller was expected to start at quarterback for

Flacco was called on to start for the Baltimore Ravens during his rookie season in 2008.

the Baltimore Ravens. But he was lost for the season due to shoulder surgery. So Flacco was forced to learn on the job.

As expected, Flacco struggled early on. He bottomed out during a three-game losing streak. The worst was a 31–3 loss to the Indianapolis Colts. Flacco threw three interceptions, lost a fumble, botched a handoff, and got sacked four times in that game. The loss lowered the Ravens' record to 2–3.

Football fans are not patient. They began to criticize the Ravens for drafting Flacco. The quarterback had a lot of pressure placed on him. But he responded. Flacco led his team to an 11–3 record the rest of the year. The Ravens even made the playoffs.

Flacco revealed many interesting facts about himself in a 2009 story in the *Baltimore Sun*. For instance, one of his brothers nicknamed him "Melonhead" as a kid. The name originated because he had such a big head for his skinny body. Flacco also said his favorite movie is *Gladiator*. And he eats pancakes and bacon before games.

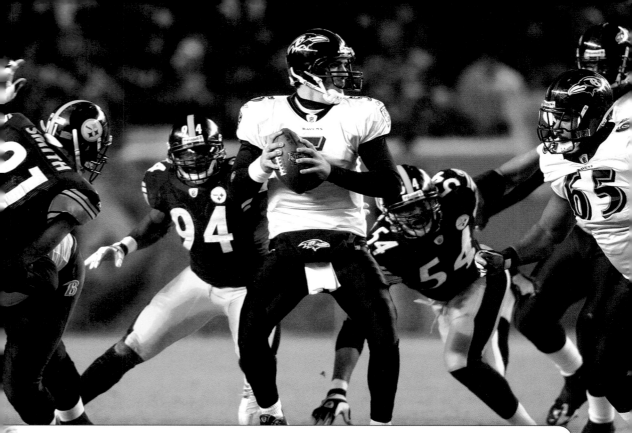

Pittsburgh Steelers defenders close in on Flacco during the January 2009 conference title game.

Baltimore came within one win of the Super Bowl. But Flacco played poorly in the playoffs. He completed just 44 percent of his passes. He also tossed three interceptions in the conference championship game against the archrival Pittsburgh Steelers. That was the Ravens' third loss to the hated Steelers in 2008, and many blamed Flacco.

Joe Flacco

Flacco made his NFL debut in 2008 against the Cincinnati Bengals. He passed for just 129 yards and no scores in the win. But he did scamper 38 yards for a touchdown. That was the longest touchdown run by a quarterback in Ravens history. The record surprised many. After all, Flacco is generally not a major threat as a runner.

The same story played out over the next three seasons. Flacco continued to lead the Ravens into the playoffs. But they kept falling short of the Super Bowl. Still, Flacco was growing as a quarterback.

He also was growing as a person. Flacco understood his responsibility of being a role model to kids. He involved himself in the Special Olympics for physically challenged children and adults. He also participated in the Polar Bear Plunge. At that event, Flacco jumped into the icy waters of the Chesapeake Bay in the middle of winter to raise money for that charity.

Flacco did the Polar Bear Plunge into the Chesapeake Bay in January 2011 to raise money for the Special Olympics.

Flacco gave out Thanksgiving baskets to the needy and visited hospitals, as well. He helped in a drive to provide coats to homeless people. And he attended an event run by teammate Ed Reed to promote youth fitness. But Ravens fans judged Flacco most for his results on the field.

Flacco had proven to be very consistent. He threw for at least 3,600 yards and 20 touchdowns in his second, third, and fourth seasons. The Ravens also reached the playoffs in each of Flacco's first four seasons. They even reached the conference title game again in 2011. But they continued to fall short of the championship.

Football fans often place more blame on the quarterback than any other player. Baltimore fans were no exception.

Most teenage couples do not end up getting married. Joe and Dana Flacco were exceptions. They began dating as Audubon High School classmates. They remained together for nine years before their wedding in June 2011. Dana gave birth to son Stephen a year later. The boy was named after Joe's father.

Flacco looks for an open receiver during a 2011 game against the Indianapolis Colts.

They were growing impatient with Flacco. They did not want to wait much longer for him to win a Super Bowl. Luckily, they would not have to. The magical 2012 season was about to begin.

Joe Flacco

CHAPTER 4

SUPER SEASON

It was April 2012. The NFL season had been over for two months. And a new one was just five months away. Sports fans in Baltimore were thinking more about the upcoming Orioles baseball season than they were about Flacco and the Ravens. That is, until Flacco gave a surprising radio interview. Flacco's agent had claimed that Flacco was one of the NFL's top five quarterbacks. The radio host asked Flacco for his opinion.

Flacco tries to get a pass away under pressure during a 2012 game against the Denver Broncos.

"I think I'm the best," he said. "I don't think I'm top five, I think I'm the best."

Fans were shocked. Media members were shocked. They all had the same message for Flacco: prove it. And to prove it, he had to do something the truly elite quarterbacks had done: lead his team to the Super Bowl title.

The 2012 season started like Flacco's previous three. He played well during the regular season. And he led his team to the playoffs. But Flacco was not spectacular.

Then, suddenly, Flacco caught fire when the postseason began. The Ravens opened against the Indianapolis Colts. Flacco passed for 282 yards and two touchdowns. Baltimore won easily, 24–9. Next up was a road game against the heavily favored Denver Broncos.

The Ravens sputtered into the 2012 playoffs. They had begun the season with a 9–2 record. Then they lost four of their last five games. They had to beat the tough New York Giants in Week 16 to confirm their spot in the playoffs.

Flacco runs away from two Denver Broncos defenders during their dramatic playoff game in January 2013.

The Ravens kept it close. With 31 seconds left, the Broncos led by a touchdown. Then Flacco threw a 70-yard touchdown pass to wide receiver Jacoby Jones. The Ravens went on to win 38–35 in double overtime. Flacco threw for 331 yards and three touchdowns in the game.

That put Flacco and the Ravens in a familiar position. They were one game away from the Super Bowl. And they had to go

Flacco raises the Vince Lombardi Trophy as Super Bowl champion after his Ravens won Super Bowl XLVII.

on the road to play the powerful New England Patriots to get there. But this time, Flacco and the Ravens did not fall short.

Flacco threw three touchdown passes in the second half. Baltimore shocked the Patriots with a 28–13 win. The first mission was accomplished. Flacco had led the Ravens into the Super Bowl. Now he had to win it.

The San Francisco 49ers were favored in Super Bowl XLVII. But Flacco was determined to lead his team to a title. He tossed a 13-yard touchdown pass to wide receiver Anquan Boldin. He fired a 1-yard scoring strike to tight end Dennis Pitta. He added a 56-yard touchdown bomb to Jones. And it was still the first half! The Ravens led from beginning to end to win 34–31.

Flacco's playoff run was one of the best in NFL history. He had passed for 1,140 yards with 11 touchdowns and no interceptions. Then he was named the MVP of the Super Bowl.

The young man from a small town in New Jersey had proven that, at least in 2012, he was indeed the best quarterback in the NFL.

A Super Bowl triumph paid off big for Flacco. He signed the largest contract in NFL history in March 2013. The Ravens agreed to pay him $120.6 million over six years. That is an average of more than $20 million per season.

FUN FACTS AND QUOTES

- Joe Flacco proved that he had one of the strongest arms in the nation while he was at the University of Delaware in 2008. He won the longest distance throw competition at the College Football All-Star Challenge with a 74-yard heave. He beat out future NFL star Matt Ryan in the process.

- Flacco's calm demeanor helped keep him out of trouble in high school. He spent enough time studying to earn a 3.99 grade-point average entering his senior year. He ranked twenty-fourth in his class of 158 students.

- "He fears nothing. That's the thing about him. He really has no fear of anything. He's as tough as he can be. He's fearless in terms of taking chances. And he's going to squeeze that ball, but yet he's very, very smart." —*Ravens offensive coordinator Jim Caldwell* after Super Bowl XLVII

- Flacco has earned the nickname "Joe Cool" for his calm demeanor on the field. The moniker was not original. It was first given to Pro Football Hall of Fame quarterback Joe Montana. He boasted the same qualities. Flacco is known as "The General" to his Ravens teammates.

WEB LINKS

To learn more about Joe Flacco, visit ABDO Publishing Company online at **www.abdopublishing.com**. Web sites about Flacco are featured on our Book Links page. These links are routinely monitored and updated to provide the most current information available.

GLOSSARY

agent
A person who represents a player in off-field business.

archrival
The opponent that brings out the most emotion in a team, its fans, and its players.

charity
Money given or work done to help people in need.

contract
An agreement between a team and a player that determines the player's salary and length of commitment with that team.

draft
An annual event in which NFL teams select the top college football players.

overtime
An extra session of football played when the game is tied after four quarters.

redshirted
Spent a season practicing but not playing in games. This allows a college player to earn experience while not giving up eligibility.

rookie
A first-year player in the NFL.

scholarship
Financial assistance awarded to students to help them pay for school. Top athletes earn scholarships to represent a college through its sports teams.

scout
A talent evaluator for a college athletic program or professional sports team often responsible for signing prospective players.

transfer
To leave one school and join another.

INDEX

FURTHER RESOURCES

Krumenauer, Heidi. *Joe Flacco*. Hockessin, DE: Mitchell Lane Publishers, 2009.

Jasner, Andy. *Baltimore Ravens*. Edina, MN: ABDO Publishing Co., 2010.

Wilner, Barry. *The Super Bowl*. Minneapolis, MN: ABDO Publishing Co., 2013.